The Magnificent Blue Butterfly

Written by: Tony and Amanda Johnson

Illustrated by: Jenna Crump

Dedication

To Elle, Kayleigh, Mikey and Millie,
thank you for all of the ways you inspire me.
I love you always!

There once was a caterpillar born with no care.
The world was his oyster, he could travel anywhere!

But this caterpillar was different, his hobbies unique.
In just a short time he found that puzzle pieces were
his choice game in hide and seek.

His friends all laughed as he scoured the forest floor.
Wooden pieces did he find, not sure what puzzle they were for.

Slowly but surely puzzle pieces did he find.
But there came a period where he had to stop
and pause for a time.

You see caterpillars don't just stay caterpillars;
they transform and are unique.

They grow into something beautiful.
Keep reading if you want to take a peek!

Resting in his cocoon of comfort,
the caterpillar dreamed of his game.

He promised himself that once he got out,
more puzzle pieces would come his way!

At last, the day had come where the caterpillar broke
from his rest. He stretched his wings and
realized he had transformed into a butterfly!
His little heart beat in his chest!

The caterpillar... I mean butterfly,
had no time to spare!

Of course, he had new beautiful wings,
but a puzzle did he dream of solving so rare!

The butterfly used his new flight to scour for pieces,
a mystery he needed to solve. The monkeys and
the snakes hissed and shouted that the butterfly's passion
was useless, too much time did this search involve.

But the butterfly persisted and in a short time,
the puzzle was complete.
Drenched in fabulous colors the animals
from across the jungle came to see.

"Oh!" exclaimed the other animals,
we have never seen something so beautiful!

"The true beauty is that I never gave up!" squeaked the
butterfly, along with a shake of his head so dutiful.

The butterfly took a step back to gaze at his work.
The final picture was a beautiful blue butterfly,
it was him! He realized with a jerk!

"What beautiful wings!
A color so blue!

This whole time I was searching for myself!
I am the puzzle" the butterfly thought as he flew.

Well now that I am complete,
but my time here is limited,
I want to help the forest, there are
so many animals in my adventures
that I have visited.

Though the butterfly's days were numbered,
kindness did he share. No longer did he search for
missing pieces, his heart filled with so much care.

And so the tale of the butterfly lives on to this day.
His story is unique, just like yours.
Take this as a sign to continue on your way!

Your colors are special and your interests are too.
There are countless ways that you can change the world,
and it all starts with your view.

This book is inspired by the Secret Blue Butterfly, a movement with the intention of spreading love and kindness throughout the world via the symbol of the magnificent butterfly. Founder, David Ahearn, offered this tremendous testimonial: "How appropriate that this book captures not only the spirit of our movement, but more importantly, gives our children the foundation to create a kinder and more loving generation of citizens. This book illustrates that the power is within us all to create a more harmonious world."

To learn more about the
Secret Blue Butterfly,
visit: www.secretbluebutterfly.com

About the Authors

Tony and Amanda Johnson own Mindful and Fit Coaching, a family wellness brand with a mission to provide young families with integrated tools and strategies that touch their hearts, heal their hurts, and give them solid footing as they transform their lives from the inside out.

Mindful and Fit Coaching has inspired hundreds of people to pursue optimal health and wellness by offering best practices in mindfulness-based stress reduction, nutrition, and breath-to-movement exercise. Our brand and work has been featured on the Doctors Television Show, in People Magazine, and on several podcasts including The Impact Show by Todd Durkin.

Tony is an author, college professor, personal trainer, and motivational speaker, and Amanda is an author, yoga instructor, and an Ayurvedic chef. Both of us are trained practitioners of meditation and parents to two beautifully unique and miraculous baby girls named Emory and Ellie. We are inspired to help bring Eastern Philosophical practices to help families live healthy and fulfilling lives.

In order to learn more about our online and in-person offerings, including our self-directed courses, coaching opportunities, and family wellness retreats please visit: www.mindfulandfit.io

About the Illustrator

Jennafer Crump is a mom and Graphic Design Student at College of the Mainland in Texas City, TX.

In addition to her work as a Graphic Artist and Illustrator, Jenna has worked with children in many capacities over the years including teaching toddler and preschool-aged children up to high schoolers. It has always been a mission of hers to help students of every age feel loved and accepted and she is thrilled to help create books that promote self-acceptance to children and families.

Growing up dancing and continuing on to train in Brazilian Jiu Jitsu as an adult, Jenna has always been passionate about knowing your body and making healthy choices. I am grateful for this opportunity to bring together so many facets of my life to create something that could be inspiring or helpful to others.